PAMPHLETS ON AMERICAN WRITERS • NUMBER 58

UNIVERSITY OF MINNESOTA

⤹ *James Gould Cozzens*

BY GRANVILLE HICKS

UNIVERSITY OF MINNESOTA PRESS • MINNEAPOLIS

© Copyright 1966 by the University of Minnesota

ALL RIGHTS RESERVED

Printed in the United States of America at the
Jones Press, Minneapolis

3 2

Library of Congress Catalog Card Number: 66-64590

The author thanks Harcourt, Brace, and World for permission
to quote from *Men and Brethren, Ask Me Tomorrow, The
Just and the Unjust, Guard of Honor,* and *By Love Possessed;*
and Mrs. James Gould Cozzens for permission to quote from
S.S. San Pedro, Castaway, and *The Last Adam.* He is grateful
to Stanley Edgar Hyman for lending him material and for
discussing some of his problems with him.

PUBLISHED IN GREAT BRITAIN, INDIA, AND PAKISTAN BY THE OXFORD
UNIVERSITY PRESS, LONDON, BOMBAY, AND KARACHI, AND IN CANADA
BY THE COPP CLARK PUBLISHING CO. LIMITED, TORONTO

NO. 58

UNIVERSITY OF MINNESOTA PAMPHLETS
ON AMERICAN WRITERS   65 CENTS

James Gould Cozzens

BY GRANVILLE HICKS

JAMES GOULD COZZENS

GRANVILLE HICKS, author of several books, both fiction and nonfiction, has for some time contributed a weekly page, "Literary Horizons," to *Saturday Review*. His latest book is his autobiography, *Part of the Truth*.

✦ *James Gould Cozzens*

Wᴴᴇɴ his first novel, *Confusion*, was published in 1924, James Gould Cozzens was in his twenty-first year and was a sophomore at Harvard College. At the time the Boston newspapers suggested that here was Harvard's reply to *This Side of Paradise* by Princeton's F. Scott Fitzgerald and *The Beginning of Wisdom* by Yale's Stephen Vincent Benét. The novel, however, was not autobiographical in the sense that the other novels were. If its theme was education, it was the education not of a young man rather like the author but that of an exotic young woman with a noble French father and a brilliant British mother. This young woman, Cerise D'Atrée, is at first educated by wise friends of her father and by extensive travels through Europe. After the outbreak of World War I she is taken to New York and exposed to a variety of upper-class American institutions. One of her mentors wonders whether Cerise's sensibility hasn't been so highly developed as to unfit her for life in the modern world, and Cozzens seems to be saying that it has.

Cozzens, born in Chicago on August 19, 1903, grew up on Staten Island, spent six years at the Kent School in Connecticut, and entered Harvard in 1922. While he was still in preparatory school he wrote an article that was published in the *Atlantic Monthly*, and he wrote *Confusion* during his freshman year in college. If he was not so sophisticated as he tried to appear, he was more sophisticated than the majority of college freshmen, and he was already developing an attitude toward life that distinguished him from his contemporaries. He was not concerned with the revolt of youth, of which both Fitzgerald and Benét were exponents, and it is probable that he would have referred to their books, as he later referred to the works of even more distinguished contemporaries, as "kid stuff." In his own immature way he was already a conservative. It would take some time, however, and many books for him to clarify his views and create a style that was appropriate to what he was trying to say. We shall have to proceed novel by novel in order to understand how the author of *Confusion* became the author of *By Love Possessed*.

The publication of *Confusion*, Cozzens has said, went to his head, and he took a year's leave of absence to write another book. This was *Michael Scarlett* (1925), a novel of Elizabethan England, which opens with an adventure at the time of the Spanish Armada. Subsequently Michael attends Cambridge University, where he meets Christopher Marlowe and Thomas Nashe, and later, in London, he enjoys the companionship not only of Marlowe and Nashe but also of Ben Jonson, John Donne, and William Shakespeare. He is himself a poet of some merit, but he has plenty of time for duals, brawls, and love affairs. Like most of the university wits, he dies an early and violent death.

Although the novel is less serious in intention than *Confusion*, and often descends to romantic claptrap, it seems to grow out of an affectionate feeling for the Elizabethan period and the writers who graced it. Moreover, in the character of Michael, Cozzens made some attempt to portray an ideal aristocrat — a man of letters but also a man of action and a romantic lover. The style is self-conscious and sometimes pretentious, but it does avoid the pseudo-antique language of Maurice Hewlett and other romantic novelists who could have influenced Cozzens. Bad in itself, the book is impressive as a kind of schoolboy exercise.

Instead of returning to college after the completion of *Michael Scarlett*, Cozzens spent a year in Cuba, tutoring the children of American engineers, and out of this experience came his next two novels. *Cock Pit* (1928) is frankly melodramatic and full of violence. The hero is Lancy Micks, chief field engineer for a large sugar company, a man quick with his fists or with a gun, a he-man through and through. His life is threatened in the course of an intra-company feud, and of course he acquits himself valiantly.

The central position in the novel, however, is occupied not by Lancy but by his daughter, Ruth, who is much like him. As a younger girl, she was hot-tempered and uncontrollable: she "had once, in unreasonable fury, horsewhipped a stable boy." Now, after a few years of education in the United States, she has acquired some discipline, but she is still independent, unconventional, and ruthless. (She does not hesitate to have her father's would-be assassin tortured until he reveals his secrets.) Several men find her attractive, but, though she likes male attention, she is in love with no one and perhaps unlikely to be. A wise old man thinks of her as "a clear head working easily among muddled ones."

The style seems less fastidious than that of the earlier books. For one thing, Cozzens goes to great length to avoid "he said": "exploded Lancy Micks," "soothed Mr. Britton," "boomed Mr. Fletcher," "pronounced Mr. Gilbert," "inquired Lancy Micks gently," "urged Mr. Arnold," "pleaded Mr. Nortz," "advised Lancy Micks," "snapped Arnold." The dialogue often seems lacking in verisimilitude, and the long conversation that Ruth has at the end with Don Miguel, the big boss, is preposterous.

The second novel about Cuba, *The Son of Perdition* (1929), marks the end of Cozzens' apprenticeship. More firmly written than any of its predecessors, it is also better constructed. All of the characters are believable, and none gets out of hand as Ruth Micks does in *Cock Pit*.

There are two stories, one concerning a group of Cubans, the other a group of Americans. Both themes are introduced in the first four chapters. Pepe Rijo, called Mono Pasmado, "a surprised monkey," is alcalde of Dosfuegos, a town completely under the control of the United Sugar Company. When we meet him, Pepe seems to be demented, his spasm having been brought on by the death of a fellow townsman named Osmundo Monaga, and by the appearance of an American vagabond, Oliver Findley, who Pepe thinks is the devil.

Cozzens drops back to show the events that led up to Pepe's panic, telling first about the Monaga family: Vidal, a proud old fisherman with the virtues of the peasant class; his son, Osmundo, a skillful builder of boats; Osmundo's sister and mistress, Nida. In the end, roused to fury, Osmundo tells his father about the relationship that exists between brother and sister.

The second theme concerns Oliver Findley, well bred and well educated, an alcoholic, a tramp, a sponger, a thief, and a cynic. He meets Joel Stellow, who is dictator over the realm of the United Sugar Company and who decides to help Findley get out of Cuba, believing that he is certain to damage the reputation of all Americans. Findley behaves so badly that Stellow has to take more drastic action. Findley meets Nida, with predictable results, and it is this incident that leads to Osmundo's revelation and his consequent death at the hands of his father.

Stellow is the kind of man Cozzens admires — cool, competent, as indifferent to conventional morality as he needs to be but no more so. An old friend, Dr. Palacíos, feels that Stellow has "the strong impersonality and intelligent ruthlessness of which all great men are made." Ultimately, however, Stellow is defeated by the proud integrity of Vidal Monaga and by the inviolable independence of Oliver Findley.

Findley, so far as Pepe and the other natives are concerned, is a feeble sort of fiend, but in Stellow's world he is truly a devil because he cannot be controlled and used. "Wherever you go there'll be trouble," Stellow tells Findley, "and it's not going to be here." By completely rejecting Stellow's values, Findley remains invulnerable. Speaking of the beating his men have given Findley, Stellow says, "You must get a lot out of it to keep on doing it." Findley replies, "I don't 'must' anything. . . . That's one thing I get out of it, Mr. Stellow."

Cozzens does not try to deal with his materials at any great depth. He treats the theme of incest almost casually, and Vidal is allowed to be offhand in describing the horrible manner in which he murdered his son. Findley, for the most part, is an amusing character rather than a demonic one. But Cozzens does certain things well. With only a few details he gives the reader a sense of the power of United Sugar. His characters, including such comparatively minor ones as Dr. Palacíos and Fray Alejandro, are endowed with a substantial degree of life, and in the many conflicts that make up the story the opponents are evenly matched. Whatever else may be true, the movement of the narrative is strong and fast.

Cozzens had still to make any strong impression on either the critics or the reading public, but with *S.S. San Pedro* (1931) he reached both, for the short novel was chosen by the Book-of-the-Month Club and was much talked about. It is the earliest book that, in recent years, he has chosen to include in his list of publications. The novel is based on the sinking of the *S.S. Vestris* on November 12, 1928, with the loss of 110 lives. Felix Riesenberg, writing in the *Nation* a fortnight later, called the captain of the *Vestris* "a study of criminal indecision," and continued, "Timidity of almost heroic proportions must have gripped him."

Captain Clendening of the *San Pedro*, who corresponds to Captain Carey of the *Vestris*, is Cozzens' central figure. Cozzens is concerned with the ship, with its officers, to some extent with its crew, and almost not at all with its 172 passengers. Even about

9

the officers we know little except with reference to their performance of their duties. Unlike Thornton Wilder's success of a few years earlier, *The Bridge of San Luis Rey*, which had examined the lives of several victims of a disaster with a view to showing what had gone before, Cozzens focuses firmly on the present.

The novel opens with the kind of succinct statement of precise facts for which Cozzens was to become famous: the tonnage of the *San Pedro*, its destination, its cargo, the number of passengers. After a brief glance at the process of loading the ship, we follow Anthony Bradell, the senior second officer, to the captain's cabin. From the first, emphasis is on Captain Clendening's air of weariness and ill health. He has with him a Doctor Percival, whom he asks Bradell to take around the ship. This gives Cozzens further opportunity to make us acquainted with the ship, but we soon realize that the doctor, who is forbidding in appearance and asks ominous questions, is an intimation of the disaster that lies ahead.

With the ship under way, we see certain officers at their work, particularly Mr. Bradell, whose duties force upon him a reluctant mingling with the passengers. As the night passes, indications multiply that all is not well with the ship. With relentless precision Cozzens describes the coming of the storm and the measures taken to resist it. By the next day Bradell is "extraordinarily tired." "In this state," Cozzens writes in a Conradian passage, "the ocean became almost personified; a purposeful and malicious agent driving its heavy assaults to the unexpected and unguarded points." As the crisis intensifies, it becomes clearer and clearer that the captain is incapable of dealing with it. Bradell does his best, which is not good enough. Clendening fatally delays the order to abandon ship, and when it sinks, he goes down with it. Bradell is presumably saved through the devotion of the quartermaster, a Brazilian of mixed blood, but we know nothing of most

of the others on board. Bradell, who has been hit by a boom, re-
covers consciousness in time to witness the sinking of the ship.

Several early reviewers of the book found it difficult to believe
that Cozzens had never been at sea except as a passenger. His
willingness to make whatever effort might be necessary to acquire
knowledge relevant to his literary aim was to remain one of his
distinguishing qualities. If the book is overwhelmingly convinc-
ing, it is because the author makes us believe in the omniscience
that many novelists assume but fail to validate.

With the air of omniscience goes a kind of objectivity that
chills the emotions of the reader, so that one is not greatly dis-
turbed by the calamity. And yet Cozzens exerts himself to make
Clendening a sympathetic person. According to the article by
Felix Riesenberg, Captain Carey of the *Vestris* was worrying
about the profits of the owners, but Cozzens' captain is old and
ill and unlucky and much concerned with death. At the outset
he wonders "how many more voyages he would be good for, and
what would be left then but death, so slow, so horribly swift." As
the gale strikes the ship, he says to Bradell, "You don't like going
out, boy. Sort of cold. Sort of lonely. Well, we all got to do it."
When the ship is foundering, and he is "quietly aware of death
like a man beside him," he shrinks from his doom, but then a
kind of numbness enables him to meet death in the manner pre-
scribed for his profession. Not a heroic character, he is touch-
ingly human.

The only disturbing element in the book is the role played by
Doctor Percival. At the beginning, as I have said, we are made to
see him as a man of ill omen. Later one of the passengers, the
flirtatious Marilee, asks Bradell if the "old gentleman in black" is
still aboard. When he tells her that the doctor went ashore, she
says, "That's fine. . . . I thought I saw him tonight. He gave
me the willies. I'm not fooling you, Bradell. I darn near marched

ashore. I'll bet I'll see him in my dreams. You don't suppose he was dead, do you?" And at the end, lying stunned in a lifeboat, Bradell has a vision of a man "in a shabby black overcoat" — "the fleshless face was steady and close, brooding on them." One has to ask whether a symbol such as this is justified in a book that is otherwise so solidly realistic.

With *S.S. San Pedro*, Cozzens was on his way, and it seemed likely that he would travel far, but his readers were not prepared for the stride he took in *The Last Adam* (1933). This is a novel about life in a small town, called New Winton, in Connecticut, but it is not an attack on the small town in the manner of Sinclair Lewis' *Main Street*, which had been published thirteen years earlier. As Cozzens knows and shows, there are skeletons in many New Winton closets, but he takes them as much for granted as the gossip in the postoffice or the confusion at a town meeting. Although this is one of the best novels about small-town life ever written, the small town is not its principal subject. New Winton is simply the background for a drama of some force, but Cozzens likes to make his background solid, and by this time he knew how to achieve solidity by the economic use of observed facts.

Our introduction to New Winton is by way of a telephone operator named May Tupping. May, it should be pointed out, is not a mere expository convenience but a person whose reflections contribute to the richness of the novel. She is useful, however, and Cozzens skillfully uses her to introduce most of the important characters and to point to certain critical issues. Soon we begin to feel that we know the town. Cozzens' adroit analysis of the class structure might well have been admired by J. P. Marquand. Cozzens knows what is the most important aspect of social distinctions in a small town: "Since no one, by his behavior, gave the faintest sign of considering himself inferior to any one else, these were subtleties you had to recognize by long acquaintance."

But if New Winton is brought to life for us, what really engages our attention is a country doctor, appropriately named Bull. Because Cozzens later wrote a novel about a lawyer and another about a clergyman, critics sometimes said of him that he was making a study of the professions. But *The Last Adam* is not a novel about a doctor in the sense that *Arrowsmith* is. Because his hero happened to be a doctor, Cozzens characteristically acquired enough information about medicine to ensure the accuracy of detail on which he prides himself, but Bull is not and is not meant to be a representative physician, as Cozzens makes clear by contrasting him with the young, up-to-date, fashionable Doctor Verney.

Bull is a maverick, in medicine as in all other ways. He is sensual, malicious, defiant, an unsubduable egoist. No rebel in the ordinary sense, anything but a political radical, he is constitutionally opposed to people in power and to all people who think they are better than other people. He is happily a thorn in the flesh of the Bannings, the town's richest and most pretentious family. Highly vulnerable because of his unprofessional behavior and his defiance of the local sexual mores, he defends himself by striking at his enemies by any means available, and his enemies are numerous. Whatever he does, he does with his whole being, whether he is catching rattlesnakes, making love, cursing out the town fathers, or trying to cope with a typhoid epidemic.

There are other characters of some interest. Herbert Banning is the exact opposite of Bull, a man so reasonable that he is incapable of action. Bullied by his wife, unable to deal with his spoiled, irrational children, he can only meditate upon the reasons for his impotence, but he is not without his admirable qualities. Between Bull and Banning stands Henry Harris, who is no more given to acting on impulse than Herbert Banning but who knows exactly how to act in his own interests and who has become not only well-to-do but also a political force. Cozzens writes of him: "As well as a native, half-knavish wit, his was that careful mean shrewdness by which alone a man can climb, not too visibly soiled, through the sewer-like lower labyrinth of American politics." In the end his wit saves Doctor Bull, not because he loves Bull but because he detests Mrs. Banning.

But of course Bull dominates the book. Janet Cardmaker, his mistress for many years, sums him up: "There was an immortality about him, she thought; her regard fixed and critical. Something unkillable. Something here when the first men walked erect; here now. The last man would twitch with it when the earth expired. A good greedy vitality, surely the very vitality of the world and the flesh, it survived all blunders and injuries, all attacks and misfortunes, never quite fed full. She shook her head a little, the smile half derisive in contemptuous affection. Her lips parted enough to say: 'The old bastard!' "

Unlike other of Cozzens' books, this novel has a good deal of humor — the boisterous humor of Bull, the wisecracking of Henry Harris, the comedy of a school pageant. But what really sets the novel apart is the role played by Doctor Bull. There are plenty of mavericks in Cozzens' work, but usually they come to bad ends, and often they are contrasted with the men of reason who are his heroes. Although Cozzens does justice to the reasonable Herbert Banning, his sympathy — surprisingly, it now seems — is with Doctor Bull.

The year after *The Last Adam*, Cozzens published his least characteristic novel, *Castaway* (1934). The novel, as the epigraph makes clear, is about a modern Robinson Crusoe. A man, never called anything but Mr. Lecky, in flight but we do not know from what, finds himself in the basement of a large department store. Why the store is empty and why it remains empty for the several days covered by the story we are not told either directly or through the thought processes of Mr. Lecky; Cozzens simply asks us to accept the situation as given.

Mr. Lecky's first concern is to protect himself against mysterious and perhaps imaginary enemies, and Cozzens follows in careful detail his search for weapons of defense. As Mr. Lecky goes on to look for shelter and food, we realize how inept he is. He is the modern unself-reliant man; unlike Crusoe, who made so much of little, he has great difficulty in making little out of much. The effectiveness of the early chapters depends on the precision with which Cozzens imagines and portrays the castaway's struggles. Climbing seven flights of stairs becomes an ordeal comparable to the pioneers' crossing of the Rockies.

Eventually there is a Man Friday, footprints and all, but Mr. Lecky, in terror, kills him. As his physical needs are taken care of, the castaway's psychological problems multiply. He is at times lonely, bored, irrationally frightened, reverting to the terrors of childhood. His mind rapidly deteriorates, finally reaching such a state of confusion that the end of the book is difficult to interpret.

On the surface, as has been said, the novel is a portrayal of the helplessness of modern man, dependent on machines that he does not know how to manage. It may also be a parable of the Depression, of a society perishing in the midst of abundance. More fundamentally, however, it is a study of poverty of mental rather than physical resources. Stanley Edgar Hyman has compared the book with Kafka's works, and has said, "It is in the tradition of the American supernatural story, the moral allegories of Hawthorne and Henry James." Cozzens had written nothing like it before and has written nothing like it since.

In *Men and Brethren* (1936), instead of repeating or carrying further the experiment he had attempted in *Castaway*, Cozzens returned to the method he had employed in *The Last Adam* — a realism based on the highly selective use of specific details. It is more accurate to call *Men and Brethren* a novel about a clergyman than it is to describe *The Last Adam* as a novel about a doctor. That is, his being a clergyman is the most important thing about Ernest Cudlipp, whereas the most important thing about Doctor Bull is his rebellious vitality. On the other hand, *Men and Brethren* is a novel about a minister, not, in the fashion of *Elmer Gantry*, a novel about the ministry.

The action in *The Last Adam* takes place in exactly four weeks; the action in *Men and Brethren* takes place in less than two days. They are two crowded days in the life of the Reverend Ernest Cudlipp, vicar of Saint Ambrose's, an Episcopal chapel in a poverty-stricken section of New York City. Let me enumerate the activities in which Cudlipp is involved: (1) He has dinner with an old and rather too affectionate friend, who has quarreled with her husband. (2) He arrives at the apartment of a young woman just in time to prevent her from committing suicide and arranges for her to have an abortion. (3) Back at the vicarage, he talks with his superior, who forbids him to allow a rabbi to speak in the chapel, and with a young assistant who is simultaneously flirting with Communism and Buchmanism. (4) A parishioner, an alcoholic in desperate condition, comes to his office, and he secures help for her. (5) A classmate calls Cudlipp to say that he has broken with the High Church order to which he has been devoted. Cudlipp invites him to spend the night but refuses to talk with him. (6) The next morning he does talk with the man, who is in disgrace because of the discovery of his homosexuality, and gives him sound but unappreciated advice. (7) He secures a Roman Catholic priest for a woman of the neighborhood who is dying. (8) He has to deal with the problems of an irresponsible young poet whom he has tried to befriend. (9) He learns that the woman alcoholic has drowned, probably by intention. (10) He quarrels with the homosexual, who strikes him and calls him a hypocrite. (11) He reads a dull sermon written by his goodhearted but stupid curate. (12) He comforts the woman who has had an abortion.

Cozzens is almost alone among his contemporaries in having written sympathetically about a clergyman. Cudlipp is unconventional enough to worry his superiors, but essentially he is, like Cozzens himself, a conservative. At one time, Cudlipp admits, he was "passionately, priggishly, broad-minded and liberal," but he has got over that. He has had much experience, he tells one of the persons he is trying to help, with "cheap people." "As far as I'm given grace to," he explains, "I try to love them, since in God's sight they are precious. I do what I can for them. It isn't much, because there is usually little to work on. . . . Many of them seem to be simply bad stock, bad blood — just what those things really are doesn't matter. . . . The matter is practical, not theoretical. They have no chance because they are no good. Why they are no good is another matter, not relevant at this point."

For Cudlipp, as for many of Cozzens' heroes, common sense is a major virtue. His argumentative assistant, speaking of a man who has just been jailed, says, "He's the natural product of a society in which property is the source of privilege — until we change that, we won't get anywhere." Ernest replies: "Until we get somewhere, how will we change that? . . . Your friends downtown aren't getting anywhere, Wilber. They're sentimentalists. They don't believe in the doctrine of original sin. Realists are the only people who get things done. A realist does the best he can with things as they are. Don't waste your time trying to change things so you can do something. Do something, do your Christian duty, and in time you may hope things will change." Thinking about the young man, Cudlipp reflects: "As far as his intention enabled him to be, he was perfect in the first-named fruit of the spirit. What more could you ask of any man? You could ask better sense!"

One cannot very well write about a clergyman without raising theological questions. Of his own religious views Cozzens has said only that he was brought up an Episcopalian. One gets the impression that he is a skeptic but, like Arthur Winner's father in *By Love Possessed*, would think it bad taste to make much of his skepticism. At any rate Ernest Cudlipp is a forthright Christian, and Cozzens appears to respect his orthodoxy. Reflecting on the popularity of Karl Barth's books in the seminaries, Cudlipp decides that "the really valuable thing Doctor Barth did seem to offer was a conception of religious truth which allowed modern-minded young priests like Wilber to recover that sustaining, snobbish ease of mental superiority, loved long since, but, fifty or sixty years ago, lost to the clergy for a while. In these well-cut, stylish new clothes, God could be introduced to any company without embarrassment." At the end, talking to the woman who has had an abortion, Cudlipp speaks of his decision to enter the ministry. It had been arrived at by a kind of accident: "In short, the Church gave me an opening." Distressed, she asks if that was all. Smiling, he asks, "Isn't it enough? . . . It seems to me to be. It's the best way to tell it. It can be understood by people who are satisfied with chance as a sufficient cause. To those who have faith in the miraculous, and believe that there is a purpose in the world, it is just as purposeful and miraculous as the conversion of St. Paul."

There is another problem that Cozzens has to face and does face: Cudlipp's chastity. Cozzens knows that many readers, under Freudian influence, will suspect that the vicar is at least latently homosexual, and he does not deny this possibility. He speaks of Cudlipp's dependence on his mother, alludes to a rumor that he was "unduly interested in young men," and mentions, though in

18

a tentative way, his "psychological aversion to women." But, since Cudlipp is not overtly homosexual and is chaste, Cozzens is not concerned with what may be going on in his subconscious.

To Cozzens, Cudlipp is simply a man doing a job and, all things considered, doing it well. In this respect he foreshadows the Cozzens heroes to come — Abner Coates, Colonel Ross, and Arthur Winner. He is not quite so stolid as they, but he would like to be.

Before he went on to Coates and the others, Cozzens had in *Ask Me Tomorrow* (1940) another kind of hero to deal with, a very different sort of person and of special interest because he seems to bear some rather intimate resemblance to Cozzens himself. This is Francis Ellery, who, at twenty-three, has written a couple of novels and is living abroad. (Cozzens spent the year 1926–27 in Europe.) Whether or not the novel is in any strict sense autobiographical, we can assume that in it, as in nothing else he has written, Cozzens has made direct use of personal experiences.

So much being true, it is interesting to note that Cozzens did not try to make Ellery an attractive character. When we are introduced to the young man, he is leaving Florence, where he has been living with his mother, to take a job as tutor in Montreux. His mother asks him to look out for a girl named Faith Robertson, who will be on the train. "I wish you could be pleasanter to people, darling," she says. "I think she was rather taken with you the other day." He replies, "I wasn't much taken with her," and goes on, "These musicians! They're all simply insufferable. Like actresses. There's always something wrong with a person who performs in public." Soon after his encounter with Faith, he says, "I think Milan's one of the most boring cities in the world," and since she disagrees, saying, "I always think it's one's own fault if one's bored," they get off to a bad start. She remarks on his touchiness, and says, "Why can't you be natural? . . . Why do you bother to try to cut a figure?" He shows off, making many literary allusions, and she threatens to leave the car when he talks coarsely and scornfully of women. Later they get on better, partly because she knows a girl in Paris, Lorna, in whom he is interested, and he takes her to dinner in Milan. Ellery gets a little tight, and, as Cozzens delicately puts it, "physical urgency flooded his body in a vast impatience, recommending to his mind the idea or image of Miss Robertson's female body." But the urgency is not strong enough to overcome both her reluctance and his. When they separate, she says, "Tomorrow we'd both be sorry. It isn't worth it." He manages to say, in his "lofty manner," "The reflexes have reasons that the heart knows not of," but he realizes that she is right.

The boy Ellery is to tutor is twelve-year-old Walter Cunningham, lamed by infantile paralysis and a victim of asthma. Mrs. Cunningham is rich, well educated, beautifully mannered, and relentlessly domineering. Ellery foresees difficulties, but he likes Walter reasonably well, and Walter likes him. Moreover, Mrs. Cunningham can be kind as well as bossy.

Cozzens makes no effort to conceal or mitigate Ellery's prejudices. When Ellery quarrels with a hotel proprietor, his anger swells "to a blaze of contempt for the whole monkey house of Europe and Europe's mostly undersized, jabbering, mostly not quite clean inhabitants. In this view, all was lumped together, a year's accumulation of passing annoyances and small disgusts — the shoddy posturing bombast of the new Italy. . . . La Belle France with its savage avarice and all-pervasive smell of urine; the belching, blockheaded Germans — why should anyone have any patience with any of them?" In a kind of survey of the European scene, Ellery comes to Russia: "Where, for instance, was Trotzky tonight? Francis tried to think of him, too; of the tailor's body like a dwarf in its Cossack's greatcoat, of the hope and fear, the love and hate, behind the screwed-up Jewish comedian's face, brooding (in ever deadlier personal peril as, his great services forgotten, enemies in his party worked to pull him down) on the havocs and ecstasies of the Soviet apocalypse — the Byzantine treachery, the torture chambers, the spies in the wall, the concealed revolvers, the monster parades, the waving red flags, the broken furniture and the frozen plumbing. Like scenes from Gulliver's Travels, all day and all night a double column serried past the mummy of Lenin; and in the factories the moron mechanics sang as they ruined the new machines; and in the fields the peasants like Nebuchadnezzar ate grass; and in crowded halls a thousand commissars shouted speeches; and in a thousand frowzy committee rooms the illiterate architects of the future scratched for lice and made mistakes in arithmetic as they tinkered with their millennium."

The Cunninghams move to the south of France, where Ellery again sees Lorna, but he has little chance to continue the courtship begun in Paris. Through a series of unfortunate incidents, he displeases Mrs. Cunningham, and there is a major crisis when Walter has an almost fatal attack of asthma.

Ellery has grown increasingly impatient with Lorna because he has had no opportunity to talk with her privately, and just before Walter's seizure they have a quarrel, in which, as he immediately realizes, he behaves badly. "It was not by any means the first time that, angry or resentful, he had, for little reason and that not good, said what it was stupid to say and done what it was foolish to do." There is a reconciliation after Walter's crisis, and Ellery asks Lorna to marry him. His words and his manner are not calculated to sweep a young woman off her feet, and Lorna understandably hesitates. Finally, after observing that it's been a hell of a day, she says, "Ask me tomorrow — I mean, if you still want to." But we know and she must know that, once he has had a chance to think calmly about the practical objections to a marriage, he will not repeat his proposal. His well-stocked mind brings consolation from Michael Drayton: "Since there's no help, come let us kiss and part." But they don't even kiss.

Before this, meditating on his degree of responsibility for Walter's condition, Ellery lets "his disgusted mind [wander] its ugly and futile way. He thought of the doctor, whose manner with Walter, whose sympathy and intelligence, had been so different from what Francis wildly expected; and yet (how mean and petty to think of it; how impossible not to notice it) the collar, or neckband, or whatever it was, of the shirt worn under his tunic could be seen inside the uniform collar, and it was greasy with dirt. Recoiling in disgust from human beings, you had to recoil, in another disgust, from your own recoiling; and so it went; and after years of distaste, with little done and nothing not somehow spoiled, you could look forward to the appropriate rewarding of patience or effort. You would be old — like Mr. McKellar, with everything going, so that wit began to labor, elegances grew grotesque or sinister, zest for life creaked at the joints — nearly a joke. And then, perhaps, you could hope to grow into an outright joke, like the Admiral at Grindelwald, with everyone secretly laughing; and then (far past a joke, a horror) you might enjoy the longevity of that old man, what was his name, his mother's acquaintance . . ."

These are dark thoughts for a man in his middle twenties, and they are not the expression of a passing mood. It is no wonder that Ellery, just a few minutes later, makes his proposal to Lorna less than romantic. Ellery is not romantic, and even "physical urgency" does not carry him far. At the end of the novel he is again in favor with Mrs. Cunningham, and is running away from Lorna. What will happen to him we do not know; perhaps he will write some good books, and probably he will marry, but not out of passion.

As I have said, Cozzens does not try to make Ellery likable, and Ellery does not even like himself. Cozzens may have been reacting against the glamorous expatriates that figured in the novels of Hemingway and Fitzgerald; this, he may have said to himself, is what life was really like for one American writer in the twenties. Insofar as the novel is autobiographical, it suggests that even at the beginning of his career Cozzens was very different from the writers who have made the decade famous. It also suggests that he was unsparing in self-analysis, that he sought to conceal his faults neither from himself nor from others.

In *The Just and the Unjust* (1942) Cozzens returned to life in a small town, but this time the town was located in eastern Pennsylvania. The hero is a young lawyer, Abner Coates, who has been assistant district attorney for the past four years but has just been given his first opportunity to take part in a murder case. Cozzens describes the courtroom and its occupants, emphasizing how many dull hours there are in a trial, even a murder trial. He then states the facts of the case: four men, none of them a native of Childerstown, kidnapped a dealer in narcotics and killed him; the leader of the quartet died accidentally while trying to escape from police who in fact were not looking for him; a second man has turned state's evidence; the other two are on trial.

As he had taken the trouble to learn about medicine before he wrote *The Last Adam* and about theology before he wrote *Men and Brethren*, so Cozzens made a careful study of trial law before he wrote *The Just and the Unjust*, and the extent to which he mastered the subject has amazed many lawyers. The legal details may fascinate or may bore the layman, according to his temperament, but he can be sure they are right. Furthermore, Cozzens is not being correct just because he likes to be correct, though obviously he does; it is in terms of these legal details that the novel's essential conflicts are worked out.

Although Cozzens has told us a good deal about the character of Childerstown in his description of the people in the courtroom, he goes further in his account of a barge party that takes place in the evening of the day on which the trial proper has begun. The party is being given by the Calumet Club, of which Cozzens says: "Of the four thousand odd inhabitants of Childerstown, about a hundred belonged to the Calumet Club. About thirty-eight hundred had not the least desire to belong, and if they thought about it at all, laughed not merely at the pretentious sound of calling the dances coming-out parties, but at the idea itself, with the suggestion that the course of nature waited on formal Calumet Club recognition. That left a few people who did have a desire to belong, but had not been asked. Since they considered themselves plenty good enough in all basic or important qualifications they spoke bitterly of those hoity-toity snobs. Calumet Club members thought the accusation of snobbishness absurd. Qualifications for membership were ordinary respectability and education, and some interest in the avowed objects of the club. You did not have to have money, and your grandfather did not have to have been a member. It was not their fault that most of the members were in fact children or grandchildren of former members. It was not their fault that respectability and education so often went with an adequate income. If people with means but no grandparents were congenial they were invited to join; if people with grandparents suddenly lost their means they would certainly not be invited to resign. Since giving parties was now the club's principal activity, it would be silly to have members who didn't fit it. That was all there was to it."

Accompanying Abner on the excursion is the girl he may marry, Bonnie Drummond, whom he has been taking to parties for a long time. At this point Bonnie is rather dissatisfied with Abner, and small wonder, for he is as deficient in ardor as Francis Ellery. Later on his invalid father, Judge Coates, says to Abner: "It's a good thing to be steady and level-headed; but the defect of the virtue can make you seem a little remote, or apathetic. Phlegmatic, maybe. Women don't like it." Obviously Bonnie doesn't like it, but she has been putting up with it for several years.

The party also introduces the reader to Jesse Gearhart, the local Republican boss, whom Abner distrusts as he tends to distrust all politicians. When Jesse asks him if he would like to run for district attorney, Abner is immediately uneasy, feeling that he will have to do errands for Gearhart and his friends. After worrying the point for some time, he takes his doubts to his father. Judge Coates says, "If you want to get away from them [the politicians], you'll have to get away from human society. There wouldn't be any society without them. It's attempted every now and then. Some so-called reform movement made up of people who aren't politicians sometimes wins an election. Either they learn how to be politicians pretty quick, or they don't last." Martin Bunting, Abner's boss and the man he may succeed, tells him, "Standing off and saying you don't like the way things are run is kid stuff."

Meanwhile the trial goes on, not without its surprising developments, and, as usual in Cozzens' novels, there are several secondary themes, all having some relation to the law. In particular there is the matter of a schoolteacher who has persuaded some of his students to pose for him naked. When the editor of the local newspaper tries to use the scandal as an excuse for getting rid of the school principal, Abner's sense of fair play is offended, and he is happy to find that Jesse Gearhart is on the same side. The murder trial ends with a partial disappointment for Abner, but he does resolve the problem of Bonnie and the problem of his political future.

As he had long since learned to do, Cozzens shaped the novel with precision and economy. Although the time occupied is only three days, the minor themes as well as the major ones are fully stated, developed, and brought to climax. The tone is lower pitched than in any of the earlier books, perhaps because Cozzens wanted to avoid the sensationalism so often found in fictional accounts of trials. Abner is a quiet, sensible man, almost but not quite bland, and it is not easy to get excited about him, but Cozzens does make him credible.

More explicitly than anything Cozzens had previously written, *The Just and the Unjust* defends the status quo. Abner has none of the rebelliousness to be found in Doctor Bull and, in different forms, in Ernest Cudlipp and even Francis Ellery. Yet he is not an unthinking conformist, as is shown by his distrust of Jesse Gearhart and of politicians in general. He is a man of conscience who acquires wisdom and learns to be more realistic without becoming an opportunist. He is not unaware of his shortcomings, but recognizes that they are associated with his virtues: "Though a sense of humor was generally spoken of with approval, and a man was pitied for lacking one, Abner supposed that he must lack one himself. When he saw a sense of humor in action, it always seemed to Abner a lucky thing, since somebody had to do the work of an unappreciative world, that a certain number of people could be relied on to lack it."

Although one should not hold Cozzens responsible for the opinions of his characters, it is important to note that all the more admirable characters in *The Just and the Unjust* are conservatives. Abner himself, reflecting on the men he is prosecuting, thinks: "Criminals might be victims of circumstance in the sense that few of them ever had a fair chance; but it was a mistake to forget that the only 'fair chance' they ever wanted was a chance for easy money." Again: "The rank and file [of criminals] could count on little but drudgery and economic insecurity; and for the same reason that most men in lawful pursuits could count on little else. They had no natural abilities, and lacked the will and intelligence to develop any." Martin Bunting, after telling Abner that all reformers are self-seeking crackpots, speaks of Communists. Cozzens continues: "In Cambridge Abner had seen a few people who said they were Communists. Naturally they had not bothered to explain their ideas to Abner. If they had, he would not have known what to say; they seemed queer and set apart, like poets, or homosexuals, so that it was hard to think of them as real people."

It is Judge Coates who has the last word. "Don't be cynical," he tells Abner. "A cynic is just a man who found out when he was about ten that there wasn't any Santa Claus, and he's still upset. . . . There'll be deaths and disappointments and failures," he continues. "When they come, you meet them. Nobody promises you a good time or an easy time." That civilization survives is a miracle, and that is where Abner comes in. "What do you want of me?" Abner asks. And now Judge Coates, man of reason, really does have the last word: "We just want you to do the impossible," he says.

From the beginning Cozzens has not tried to conceal his belief that the majority of people are stupid and incompetent, and he has written almost exclusively about men and women who are superior in one way or another to the masses. The only important exception is Mr. Lecky in *Castaway*, who may be regarded as a common man; but his incompetence is one of the major themes of the book. In his first two novels Cozzens portrayed European aristocrats, first of the present and then of the past; and in the Cuban novels the heroes are marked by their ability to dominate the masses of men. *S.S. San Pedro* shows what happens when a natural leader breaks down, losing the qualities on which his leadership has rested. Doctor Bull goes his own way, fortified by a good-natured contempt for most of his fellow townsmen. Ernest Cudlipp believes it his Christian duty to love "cheap people," but he knows they are "no good," and Francis Ellery, aware as he is of his shortcomings, never doubts that he is a superior person, nor does Cozzens question his assumption.

By the time he wrote *The Just and the Unjust*, Cozzens was clear as to what kind of superior man he most admired — the man of reason. Judge Coates, with his tolerance for human frailty, his realism, his distrust of emotion, his resistance to nonsense and folly, is a prime example of the man of reason. Abner, on the other hand, is only an apprentice, but he is learning, and in the course of the novel he loses some of the illusions that have kept him from growing up. He will make a man of reason in due time.

Cozzens' next novel did not appear for six years, part of which he spent in the United States Air Force, rising to the rank of major. From this experience came *Guard of Honor* (1948), which is a novel not about combat but about the military under wartime tensions. The scene is an air force base in Florida, called Ocanara, and the action takes place in three days.

Although it is the most complicated of his novels, with a large cast of characters and a great number of subplots, *Guard of Honor* is beautifully constructed, with each part in its proper place. The first chapter introduces many of the principal characters on a plane bound for Ocanara. Cozzens describes the flight with his usual precision, but the plane is important because of its passengers, and what matters is the way they reveal themselves. General Beal, Colonel Ross, Lieutenant Colonel Carricker, Captain Hicks, Lieutenant Turck (WAC), and Master Sergeant

Pellerino — these are some of the persons we are to follow through the book, and we know them reasonably well by the time they reach Ocanara. Events connected with their landing precipitate the first of the crises with which the book deals.

General Beal, the principal figure in the principal actions of the book, has to confront these crises. The first arises when, after the landing, Benny Carricker punches a Negro lieutenant. The next day the race problem becomes urgent, and on the last day several paratroopers are drowned in a celebration of Beal's birthday. As Cozzens shows him, Beal is a charming man, almost boyish in manner, a good leader of men, especially in battle, but likely to act on impulse. His closest friend is Colonel Carricker, a war hero, even more impulsive and reckless than the general.

Cozzens does not underestimate the importance in wartime of such men as Beal and Carricker, but he knows that there has to be somebody to pick up the pieces, and that is the part played by Colonel Ross, the character whom Cozzens most admires and with whom he identifies himself. Ross, a judge in civilian life, is a man of reason, and as such he strives to save Beal from the consequences of his follies.

Cozzens often tells us what is going on in Ross's mind, as, for instance, when he has been handling one of his many problems with a caution that he knows he would have scorned twenty years earlier: "Colonel Ross was not sure whether today's different attitude came from being twenty years wiser or just twenty years older. He had, of course, more knowledge of what happens in the long run, of complicated effects from simple causes, of one thing stubbornly leading to another. Experience had been busy that much longer rooting out the vestiges of youth's dear and heady hope that thistles can somehow be made to bear figs and that the end will at last justify any means that might have seemed dubious when the decision to resort to them was so wisely made.

Unfortunately, when you got to your end, you found all the means to it inherent there. In short, the first exhilaration of hewing to the line waned when you had to clean up that mess of chips. The new prudence, the sagacious long-term views would save a man from many mistakes. It was a pity that the counsels of wisdom always and so obviously recommend the course to which an old man's lower spirits and failing forces inclined him anyway."

Ross reflects that most men at Ocanara, and for that matter most people in the world, have not grown up and are engaged in a game of make-believe that they take seriously. "You found it funny or called it silly at your peril. Credulity had been renamed faith. Each childish adult determinedly bet his life and staked his sacred pride on, say, the Marxist's ludicrous substance of things only hoped for, or the Christian casuist's wishful evidence of things not so much as seen. Faiths like these were facts. They must be taken into account; you must do the best you could with them, or in spite of them." His awareness of human fallibility is the foundation of his philosophy: "There never could be a man so brave that he would not sometime, or in the end, turn part or all coward; or so wise that he was not, from beginning to end, part ass if you knew where to look; or so good that nothing at all about him was despicable." Thinking about General Nichols, Beal's superior, who by and large seems to him a wise man, Ross concludes: "To the valuable knowledge of how much could be done with other men, and how much could be done with circumstance, he might have to add the knowledge of how much could be done with himself. He was likely to find it less than he thought."

As he looks back on what he has done in the course of three days to prevent the bad from becoming worse, he thinks that it has been "a near thing, all precarious, all at hazard; no plan for it; and no theory better than anyone's good guess that the Nature of Things abhors a drawn line and loves a hodgepodge, resists consistency and despises drama; that the operation of man is habit, and the habit of habit is inertia. This weight is against every human endeavor; and always the best bet is, not that a man will, but that he won't."

If Ross is in some sense Cozzens' spokesman, there are many other characters in the book, each of them insistent on speaking for himself. Captain Hicks tries to be a man of reason and also tries to be a faithful husband, but he finds himself in bed with Amanda Turck — to the subsequent regret of both of them. Captain Duchemin, on the other hand, moves happily from bed to bed, with not a moment of remorse. And then there is Captain Andrews, a mathematical wizard, deeply and wholly in love with his wife and devastated when he thinks he must lose her.

If Cozzens is almost unique in having written sympathetically about clergymen, he is equally exceptional in treating military men of high rank with respect. Most of his characters are officers, and these officers are not seen through the eyes of a victimized private, as in so many novels of both world wars, but are taken at face value. Like all other groups Cozzens writes about, they are a mixed lot, but their being officers is not held against them.

Guard of Honor was more discussed than any of Cozzens' earlier novels had been, and in some quarters it was extravagantly praised, but there was nothing like the tumultuous reception given, nine years later, to *By Love Possessed* (1957). There were dissentient voices, the most strident being Dwight Macdonald's, but many critics called it a great novel, and within a few months more copies of it had been sold than of all Cozzens' other books put together.

Like Abner Coates and his father in *The Just and the Unjust* and Colonel Ross in *Guard of Honor*, the hero of *By Love Pos-*

sessed, Arthur Winner, is a lawyer. While Cozzens had made careful studies of several professions, it appears that the law was the most congenial to his mind, presumably because it seemed to him that the man of reason was given more scope by the law than any other profession.

The term "Man of Reason," as used by Cozzens, appears for the first time in *By Love Possessed,* and it appears there almost on the first page, when Arthur Winner thinks of his father — "the nearly unique individual; the Man, if not perfectly, at least predominantly, of Reason." He continues: "By his fruits, you knew that man. They, the many accomplishments, were for his father a simple matter. Uncluttered by the irrelevant, uncolored by the emotional thinker's futile wishing and excesses of false feeling, the mere motion of his father's thought must usually prove synonymous with, the same thing as, perfect rightness. Any end being proposed, the Man of Reason considered means. At a glance, he separated what was to the purpose from what wasn't. Thus simply, he determined the one right way to do the thing. You did it that way; and there you were."

The counter-theme has already been stated: "Love conquers all," says the scroll on the gilt clock, and there is a little scene to illustrate the maxim. Winner meditates: "Love pushed aside the bitter findings of experience. Love knew for a fact what was not a fact; with ease, love believed the unbelievable; love wished and made it so. Moreover, here where love's weakness seemed to be, love's strength resided. Itself all unreality, love was assailed by reality in vain."

Thus the issue is stated at the outset: reason versus unreason, otherwise known as love, sometimes called "feeling." For Cozzens, as for everyone else, "love" is a word that has many meanings, and the exploration of some of the meanings is one of the purposes of the novel. Like most of Cozzens' heroes in his later work, Winner is a dispassionate man. More than most men, he has lived his life in the light of reason, and at fifty-four he can legitimately take satisfaction in this achievement. The novel follows him through a period of forty-nine hours, during which he is confronted with what must be, even for him, an unusual number of difficult problems, and we are forced to respect his self-discipline, integrity, generosity of spirit, and wisdom. But Cozzens makes us understand that the life of reason is a constant struggle and that reason can never be fully triumphant.

The victories of unreason multiply as the story proceeds. A girl is brought into court, charged with murdering her newborn, illegitimate child. Young Ralph Detweiler, charged with rape, appears to have been involved with two girls. His older sister, Helen, who brought him up and dotes on him, is the faithful secretary of Winner's senior partner, Noah Tuttle. Because of her irrational devotion to the boy, Helen is thrown off balance, with far-reaching consequences. There is a political conflict and an ecclesiastical row, the latter involving a homosexual.

The irrationality of others, however, does not disturb Winner so much as the failures of his own reason. He thinks of his failure with his son Warren, who savagely rejected his father and to all intents and purposes destroyed himself. Then there are his memories of the summer after his first wife died, when he was involved in a deeply physical affair with Marjorie Penrose, wife of his partner and closest friend. Even in its most controlled form, sanctified both by marriage and affection, the sexual relationship may have unfortunate consequences: having made passionate love, on the night of that first eventful day, to his present wife, he realizes that his daughter by his first wife, whom he is trying to guide rationally through the difficult years of adolescence, has reason to suspect what has been happening.

But the wisdom that Winner hopes he has acquired is put to

an even more severe test. Winner discovers that Noah Tuttle, the man he has most admired next to his father as a model of integrity, has for several years been taking money from various funds of which he is trustee in order to protect the investors in a company that has gone bankrupt. Julius Penrose, Winner's pitifully crippled partner and the man he once cuckolded, has kept Tuttle's peculations secret for many years, and urges Winner to do the same. Otherwise, he points out, the aged Tuttle, they and their families, and many others will be injured, and for what good? Arthur, who had thought, less than forty-eight hours earlier, that it was simple for his father to decide what was the right thing to do, now realizes that issues are not so clear and decisions not so easy. He thinks of all the good advice he has given to other people in the past day or two and is now about to disregard, and he is humbled. But even at this moment, as he bitterly recognizes the limitations of reason, it is in reason that he puts his trust; fallible though it is, man has no better guide.

Even for Cozzens, *By Love Possessed* is a remarkably complicated novel, and he has handled the complications with fine craftsmanship, playing one theme against another in the most elaborate and effective kind of counterpoint. Winner's own sexual activities, for example, are compared to and contrasted with Ralph Detweiler's unfortunate experiments; the religiosity of a friend's friend and the mindlessness of a juvenile delinquent are juxtaposed; the reflections of an aged Negro with a heart condition illuminate for Winner experiences of his own and of his friends. Everything is made to count for as much as possible.

Even in the texture of the writing Cozzens goes beyond what he had done before. He has always written with complete clarity and with none of the sloppiness so often associated with what is called "the common style." Here he has developed a more elaborate prose, and, though he sometimes gets tangled up in his extremely involved sentences, he often achieves poetic power. He has endowed his principal characters with great articulateness, and, though the dialogue is no more realistic than Henry James's, he persuades us to accept it. A richness of literary allusions widens the implications of the writing, and an unobtrusive, uninsistent use of symbols points to deeper meanings.

Since the appearance of *By Love Possessed* in 1957, Cozzens has published only one book, a collection of short stories named *Children and Others* (1964), and to this it is not necessary to devote much attention. Of the seventeen stories the volume contains, thirteen were published between 1930 and 1937, most of them in the *Saturday Evening Post*. They originate, then, in the period in which Cozzens was finding himself as a novelist. All of them are competently written, but some are as slick as the paper on which they were originally printed. In particular I am bothered by some of the stories about preparatory school life, which seem to me to affirm conventional prep school values. Much the best is a recent story, not published elsewhere, called "Eyes to See," a perceptive and unusually sympathetic account of the difficult emergence from adolescence.

During his writing career, which has now extended over more than forty years, Cozzens has always stood some distance apart from his famous contemporaries. At the time he began his career the three most influential American novelists were Dreiser, Anderson, and Lewis. Cozzens' work had nothing in common with either Dreiser's clumsy naturalism or Anderson's quasi-mystical preoccupation with the inarticulate, nor did he ever show concern for the kinds of social problems that from time to time they tried to deal with. He has sometimes been compared with Lewis because both wrote of men in the professions, but Cozzens' purpose and method were completely different from Lewis'.

Although he was only a few years younger than Fitzgerald, Dos Passos, Hemingway, Faulkner, and Wolfe, his interests were not like theirs. He was never a rebel, as all of them were in one way or another. Except in *Castaway* he did not experiment with the form of the novel. He almost always wrote about man in society, not the isolated individual, usually modeled after his creator, who played so important a part in the fiction of Hemingway and Wolfe. Of the five, he was closest to Fitzgerald, who, in *The Great Gatsby* and *Tender Is the Night*, did write about man in society, but the differences in temperament were so great that the men appeared to be living in different worlds.

Except for his early romantic novels and the experimental *Castaway*, Cozzens has stayed within the bounds of the traditional social novel. Like Jane Austen, George Eliot, Anthony Trollope, Henry James, and Edith Wharton, he takes the social structure for granted, neither attacking nor defending the status quo. As a true conservative, he does not believe that whatever is is right, but he is convinced that, people being what they are, any change is likely to be a change for the worse. In any case he is not much interested in society as such but as a frame within which individuals perform their roles. Recognizing that man is a gregarious animal, he believes that men reveal themselves most fully in society.

It is often said that the traditional social novel requires a compact, homogeneous society and that such a society does not exist in the United States. In a sociological sense the latter statement is probably true, but for literary purposes serviceable substitutes may be found, as Marquand, O'Hara, and Auchincloss have shown. Cozzens has not limited himself geographically, but he has made a particular segment of the American people, the upper middle class, his kingdom. His predilection became clear in the two novels about Cuba, but it was not until *The Last Adam* that he staked out a field for himself. His small Connecticut town gave Cozzens as wide a range as he needed. There are some members of the working class, not given much prominence but treated with respect, and there are the incompetents, the bums, the *Lumpenproletariat*. But the principal characters are Doctor Bull, who, in spite of his recalcitrancy, is a member of the middle class by virtue of his profession, and Herbert Banning, who, whatever his wife might like to think, is still within the middle class, though in its highest bracket.

Men and Brethren is set in New York City, but both its geographical range and its social span are narrow. Childerstown in *The Just and the Unjust* and Brocton in *By Love Possessed* seem ideally suited to Cozzens' purposes. They are small cities rather than small towns, with a considerable upper middle class, made up of lawyers, doctors, clergymen, bankers, and a few well-to-do persons engaged in unspecified businesses. Most of these men and women belong to the older families of the community, and there are ties of kinship as well as of long-established social intimacy. The existence of the respectable working class is recognized, but its members are not important in the development of the story.

It is clear that Cozzens has no interest in farmers or factory workers, whatever the color of their collars. He has no interest in the very poor, as Dreiser and Anderson had, as Bellow and Malamud have. What is more surprising, he has no interest in the very rich and the very powerful. There are no big bankers or big industrialists in his novels, and the only politicians are on the county level. The great political crises of the past three decades are almost completely ignored, and in *Guard of Honor* the war itself plays little part. Indeed, Cozzens observes, with sardonic intent, that the conscientious Colonel Ross sometimes

37

thinks about the purpose and progress of the war, which makes him almost unique on the base.

I am not complaining about Cozzens' limitations — even Balzac and Tolstoi were limited — but I am trying to define them. All his major characters and most of his minor ones are white Anglo-Saxon Protestants. I shall comment later on his treatment of Negroes, Jews, and Catholics, but for the moment it is enough to say that they are given minor roles. If Cozzens manages to create a more or less homogeneous society, such as he needs for the sake of the kind of novel he wants to write, he does so by thrusting away from him large segments of the American people.

Cozzens has to believe, as he does believe, that the people he writes about are the people who, in broad social and moral terms, most deserve his attention. He can believe this because he is a conservative. What the man of reason, the wise man, does, as we have seen again and again, is to accept the status quo, not because it is perfect but because it is what we have to work with. Cozzens has only contempt for radicals and reformers. Ernest Cudlipp ridicules the assistant who flirts with Communism. Judge Coates and District Attorney Bunting knock the idealistic nonsense out of Abner's temporarily muddled mind. Lieutenant Edsell, the self-styled "liberal" in *Guard of Honor*, is a fool and a hypocrite.

In 1942, in one of his rare personal statements, Cozzens wrote in *Twentieth Century Authors*: "My social preference is to be left alone, and people have always seemed willing, even eager, to gratify my inclination. I am more or less illiberal, and strongly antipathetic to all political and artistic movements. I was brought up an Episcopalian, and where I live the landed gentry are Republican." One gets the impression, however, that he takes his Republicanism no more seriously than his Episcopalianism. As John Lydenberg has observed, it is difficult to imagine Cozzens as an enthusiast for either Eisenhower or Nixon, and it is even more difficult to believe that he was an admirer of Goldwater, though he may have voted for him.

Cozzens has sometimes been accused of anti-Semitism and segregationist sympathies. When, in *By Love Possessed*, a Jewish lawyer comes to Brocton, Noah Tuttle is outspokenly anti-Semitic, but his outburst is regarded by his associates as a display of bad manners. Arthur Winner's prejudice against Jews is milder and is courteously concealed from Mr. Woolf, but it does exist, and it may be that, in this as in other matters, Winner speaks for Cozzens. Whether that is true or not, it must be remembered that in the long run Woolf is seen in a favorable light.

In the same novel members of a Negro family, the Reveres, know their place, and Winner admires them for this. Critics have objected to a passage in which Cozzens tells, with approval, that Alfred Revere, who was sexton of the Episcopal Church, never took communion until the last, lest he offend white members of the congregation. But what Cozzens approves is Revere's tact, not the prejudices of the whites.

The race question is central in *Guard of Honor*, both because the base is in a southern town and because a group of Negro flyers is being trained at Ocanara. Most of the white officers are full of prejudice, talking constantly of "niggers," "dinges," and "jigaboos," and one is an articulate white supremacist. The only spokesman for the other side is the obnoxious Lieutenant Edsell, who does nothing but discredit his cause. But, though the segregationists seem to have the better of the argument, Cozzens has said that he does not believe in segregation. On the other hand, he does believe that one must always face facts, however unpleasant, and in the South racial prejudice is a fact. "We are having a little trouble with some Negro officers," Colonel Ross tells his wife. "They feel they are unjustly treated. I think in many ways they are; but there are insurmountable difficulties to doing them justice." In an interview that appeared in *Time*, Cozzens is said to have said, "I like anybody if he's a nice guy, but I've never met many Negroes who were nice guys." For that matter, he seems not to have met many white men who were nice guys. The point is that he is guilty of snobbishness rather than discrimination against Negroes.

Cozzens has also offended many Catholics. It seems clear that, though he may accept the Episcopal Church as a useful social institution, he finds religion in general full of superstition and sentimentality, and in particular he dislikes the Roman Catholic Church. "Regard that overweening hierarchy," Winner thinks; "above those mostly poor-boy bishops, elated by their local power, those impudent princes of the church — this plump, canting pudge of an eminence here; this malapert, threatening ignoramus of an eminence there! Regard that state within a state . . ." and he goes on with his indictment. To be sure, these are Winner's thoughts, not necessarily Cozzens', but Arthur's opponent, Mrs. Pratt, is quite simply a fool.

Despite whatever lip service he may pay to Episcopalianism, Cozzens appears to be a secularist of a Stoic sort. Not merely in *By Love Possessed* but in every one of his novels the role of chance is emphasized: Cerise's death in *Confusion*, the exposure of incest in *Son of Perdition*, the typhoid epidemic in *The Last Adam*, the capture of the gangsters in *The Just and the Unjust*, the death of the parachutists in *Guard of Honor*. Fate, he points out again and again, does not play fairly with us. But he does not repine, he does not protest; he simply affirms that man must prepare himself for the worst that fate can bring. He can say with Hamlet, "The readiness is all."

If nothing else distinguished Cozzens from the majority of his contemporaries, his treatment of sex would do so. In a manner of speaking, sex was discovered, for literary purposes, in the period to which Cozzens belongs: Lawrence and Joyce and Proust and most of the people who have been writing novels since them have given the sexual act a central importance it had not had in literature since the Restoration and in a way had never had. That the sexual drives are powerful Cozzens recognizes, but he seems to deny what might be called the philosophical significance of sex. In *By Love Possessed*, Winner and his second wife have sexual intercourse very pleasantly, and Cozzens describes their physical sensations in some detail, as if to prove that he, too, knows what it's all about. But for most of the characters in the novels, including Winner at one time of his life, the sexual impulse leads to disaster. Janet Cardmaker and Doctor Bull have been carrying on illicitly and happily for many years, but Bull attributes the success of the affair to the fact that it is not "at all an emotional matter." Abner Coates in *The Just and the Unjust* triumphs over his sexual impulses, but it doesn't seem much of a battle. Captain Hicks and Amanda Turck finally go to bed together, but with no great pleasure on either side. Moreover, as Stanley Edgar Hyman has pointed out, homosexuality, sadism, incest, and a kind of necrophilia are scattered through the novels. Certainly Cozzens has a right to make all he can of the less pleasant aspects of sexual experience, which have often been overlooked by novelists intoxicated with the "new freedom," but the length to which he carries his antiromanticism may be significant.

It should also be noted that few of his characters are capable of strong emotions of any kind. To be sure, he does not approve of strong emotions, but they do exist, and Shakespeare, for instance, to whose writings Cozzens is constantly alluding, was much concerned with men and women who were overcome by them. One cannot imagine Cozzens creating a Lear, a Macbeth, an Othello, or an Antony — or, for that matter, a Captain Ahab or a Joe Christmas.

Cozzens is also surprisingly indifferent to artists and the arts. Cerise in *Confusion* is educated in all the arts, and several of the characters in *Michael Scarlett* are poets, but since then Cozzens' characters, except for the more or less autobiographical Francis Ellery, have had no interest in creating art and not much in exposing themselves to it in any form. Arthur Winner, it is true, has read more widely than one would expect of a busy lawyer, but most of the writers he refers to lived before or soon after 1800. (Cozzens himself says that his models are Shakespeare, Swift, Steele, Gibbon, Jane Austen, and Hazlitt.) In 1957 *Time* wrote of Cozzens: "It is seventeen years since he and his wife saw a movie, more than twenty since they went to a theater, to a concert or an art gallery." According to the same source, he has only contempt for Hemingway, Steinbeck, Lewis, and Faulkner.

Within his limitations, which, as we have seen, are considerable, Cozzens has built a formidable career. To the traditional social novel he has brought many attributes, in particular a concern with compactness and density. By the time he wrote *Cock Pit*, he was learning to tighten his structure for the sake of dramatic effect, and in *The Son of Perdition* he skillfully managed the simultaneous development of two themes. In *S.S. San Pedro* he produced a sparse, rapid narrative but at the expense of depth of characterization. In *The Last Adam*, which covers exactly four weeks, he achieved depth, complexity, and compactness. In *Men and Brethren* the actions are quite as complicated and the span of time, less than two days, even shorter.

It is in the last three novels, however, that Cozzens has brought his method close to perfection. *The Just and the Unjust* is limited to the few days required for the trial, but in those days many things happen that tell us much about the characters. The action of *Guard of Honor*, which, we have seen, is extremely complex, takes place in three days, and the action of *By Love Possessed* in forty-nine hours. Cozzens seems to be trying to do more and more in shorter and shorter periods of time. (It is relevant to note that the novel on which he has been working for the past seven or eight years is tentatively entitled "Morning, Noon, and Night.") Each of the major characters in the later novels has a past as well as a present, and one is impressed by the way in which Cozzens, without much reliance on formal flashbacks, endows each man and woman with a history, at the same time that he explores the tangled relationships of both people and events.

According to Frederick Bracher's *The Novels of James Gould Cozzens*, Cozzens, in a letter to his English publisher about *Guard of Honor*, said: "What I wanted to write about here, the essence of the thing to be said, the point of it all, what I felt to be the important meaning of this particular human experience, was its immensity and its immense complexity. . . . I could see I faced a tough technical problem. I wanted to show . . . the peculiar effects of the inter-action of innumerable individuals functioning in ways at once determined by and determining the functioning of innumerable others — all in the common and in every case nearly helpless involvement in what had ceased to be just an 'organization' . . . and become if not an organism with life and purposes of its own, at least an entity, like a crowd." This was the kind of problem that by now he had learned to solve. The sense of complexity that John Dos Passos tried to render by a series of experimental devices in *U.S.A.* Cozzens came close to achieving within the form of a traditional novel.

Although he has never acknowledged a debt to Henry James, Cozzens has come to be as much concerned with the matter of point of view as the master himself. At first he wasn't, and he shifted his point of view without much plan. In *The Last Adam*, however, he relied chiefly on the point of view of Doctor Bull, but entered other minds as circumstances demanded. In *Guard of Honor* the consciousness of Colonel Ross is central, but the point of view moves about so that various themes can be developed simultaneously. In *By Love Possessed,* on the other hand, we enter no consciousness but Arthur Winner's, and Cozzens' success in telling so complicated a story from a single point of view might have won Henry James's admiration.

Cozzens' style in his first two novels was lush and pretentious in a juvenile way, but by the time he wrote *Cock Pit* and *The Son of Perdition* he was capable of a competent, straightforward prose, and in *S.S. San Pedro* his style was disciplined and quite adequate to the demands put upon it. In *Castaway,* as Stanley Edgar Hyman pointed out almost twenty years ago, Cozzens made a great advance stylistically, achieving a distinction of which his earlier work had shown little promise. To prove his point, Hyman quotes from this novel part of "a dissertation on the types of mania": "Let the man you meet be, instead, a paretic. He has taken a secret departure from your world. He swells amid the choicest, most dispendious superlatives. In his arm he has the strength to lift ten elephants. He is already two hundred years old. He is more than nine feet high; his chest is of iron, his right leg is silver, his incomparable head is one whole ruby. Husband of a thousand wives, he has begotten on them ten thousand children. Nothing is mean about him; his urine is white wine; his faeces are always soft gold. However, despite his splendor and his extraordinary attainments, he cannot successfully pronounce the words: electricity, Methodist Episcopal, organization, third cavalry brigade. Avoid them. Infuriated by your demonstration of any accomplishment not his, he may suddenly kill you."

Cozzens' writing has rarely been as imaginative as this, but there have been important developments as the years have gone by. His style in *Men and Brethren, Ask Me Tomorrow,* and *The Just and the Unjust* is unpretentious, sometimes slightly formal, always highly polished. He often says things neatly, and his figures of speech are sometimes effective, but on the whole his style is unobtrusive, almost transparent. All this begins to change in *Guard of Honor* and changes greatly in *By Love Possessed.* His sentence structure becomes more complicated, and his language more exotic — though he has always been fond of unusual words. His prose is no longer transparent, nor does he want it to be.

It was the style of *By Love Possessed* that Dwight Macdonald attacked most vehemently. He was not wrong all of the time, for a few of the sentences he quotes are awkwardly put together or unnecessarily involved, but much that he condemns is, in context, perfectly sound, and he ignores the many bold experiments in the use of language that prove successful. On the whole, I prefer the style of *Guard of Honor* to that of *By Love Possessed,* but the latter has virtues that should not be overlooked.

Frederick Bracher has written: "The best of Cozzens' works are evidence that the traditional social novel, with its high seriousness and moral urgency, is still viable in a period of experiment and disorder." This much is surely true. Cozzens has made the traditional novel an effective medium for the expression of his vision of life. That other novelists, with other methods and other aims, have made revelations about the human condition that seem more valuable to some of us than anything we find in his work should not persuade us to underestimate the substance and validity of what he has done.

Selected Bibliography

Works of James Gould Cozzens

Confusion. Boston: B. J. Brimmer Co., 1924.
Michael Scarlett. New York: Albert and Charles Boni, 1925.
Cock Pit. New York: William Morrow, 1928.
The Son of Perdition. New York: William Morrow, 1929.
S.S. San Pedro. New York: Harcourt, Brace, 1931.
The Last Adam. New York: Harcourt, Brace, 1933.
Castaway. New York: Random House, 1934.
Men and Brethren. New York: Harcourt, Brace, 1936.
Ask Me Tomorrow. New York: Harcourt, Brace, 1940.
The Just and the Unjust. New York: Harcourt, Brace, 1942.
Guard of Honor. New York: Harcourt, Brace, 1948.
By Love Possessed. New York: Harcourt, Brace, 1957.
Children and Others. New York: Harcourt, Brace, and World, 1964.

Current American Reprints

Ask Me Tomorrow. New York: Harbrace Modern Classics (Harcourt, Brace, and World). $2.25.
By Love Possessed. New York: Crest (Fawcett). $.95.
Castaway (with *S.S. San Pedro*). New York: Vintage (Knopf). $1.25.
Guard of Honor. New York: Harvest (Harcourt, Brace, and World). $2.45.
The Just and the Unjust. New York: Harvest. $1.95.
The Last Adam. New York: Harvest. $1.25.
S.S. San Pedro (with *Castaway*). New York: Vintage. $1.25.

Bibliography

James B. Meriwether. "A James Gould Cozzens Check List," *Critique*, 1:57–63 (Winter 1958).

Critical and Biographical Studies

Bracher, Frederick. "James Gould Cozzens: Humanist," *Critique*, 1:10–29 (Winter 1958).
————. *The Novels of James Gould Cozzens.* New York: Harcourt, Brace, 1959.

_____. "Of Youth and Age," *Pacific Spectator,* 5:48–62 (Winter 1951).

Hicks, Granville. "The Reputation of James Gould Cozzens," *College English,* 11:177–83 (January 1950).

Hyman, Stanley Edgar. "James Gould Cozzens and the Art of the Possible," *New Mexico Quarterly,* 19:476–98 (Winter 1949).

_____. "My Favorite Forgotten Book [*Castaway*]," *Tomorrow,* 7:58–59 (May 1957).

Lydenberg, John. "Cozzens and the Conservatives," *Critique,* 1:3–9 (Winter 1958).

_____. "Cozzens and the Critics," *College English,* 19:99–104 (December 1957).

Macdonald, Dwight. "By Cozzens Possessed," *Commentary,* 25:36–47 (January 1958). Reprinted in *Against the American Grain.* New York: Vintage, 1965. Pp. 187–212.

Ward, John W. "James Gould Cozzens and the Condition of Modern Man," *American Scholar,* 27:92–99 (Winter 1957–58).